PLANET EARTH

LATE INTERMEDIATE TO EARLY ADVANCED PIANO SOLOS

DENNIS ALEXANDER
PHOTOGRAPHY: PAUL DOSTERT

The world in which we live is so full of beauty and natural wonders, and we often make the mistake of taking for granted the grandeur of a waterfall or the magic of a spectacular sunset. The pictures in this collection are scenes that many of us have experienced. I have attempted to capture the music "within the pictures" by writing solos that will motivate students to play with more expression, musicality and command. As you play these solos, try to picture in your mind the photograph which accompanies each piece and allow your visual imagination to enhance your aural and technical abilities. At the same time, realize that all of us have an obligation to help preserve these natural wonders of our planet so that future generations will have the opportunity to experience these beautiful scenes!

Dennis Alexander

This collection is dedicated to Morty and Iris Manus, whose friendship and perpetual encouragement is deeply appreciated.

IN THE BEGINNING...

Glacier National Park, Montana

Commissioned by CLAVIER, April, 1991

In the Beginning...

Dennis Alexander

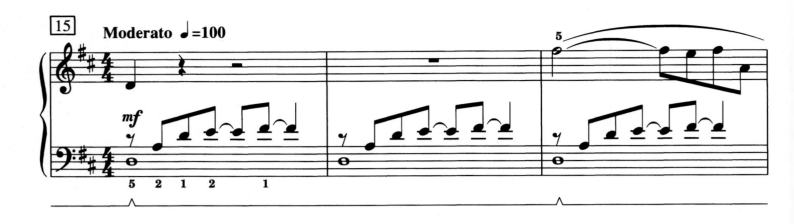

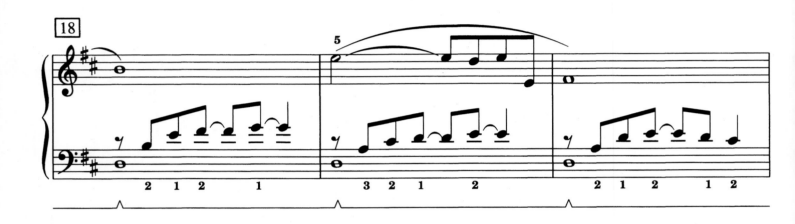

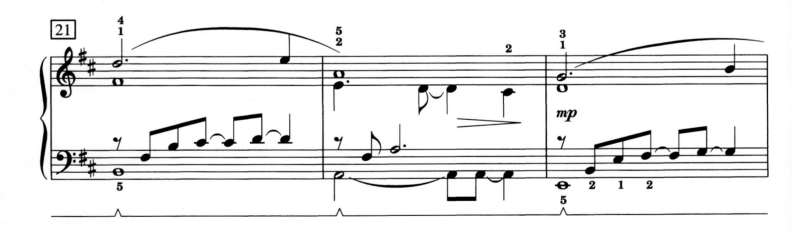

SPRING WATERS

Spring Waters

9

JESTER

Jester

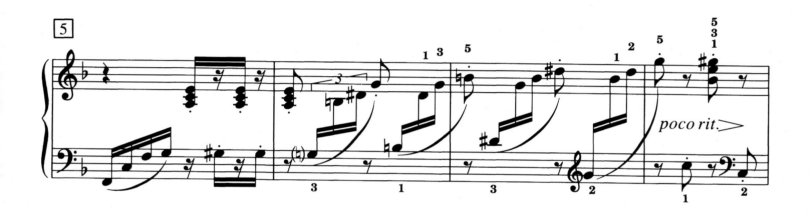

12

TURBULENCE!

Glacier National Park, Montana

Turbulence!

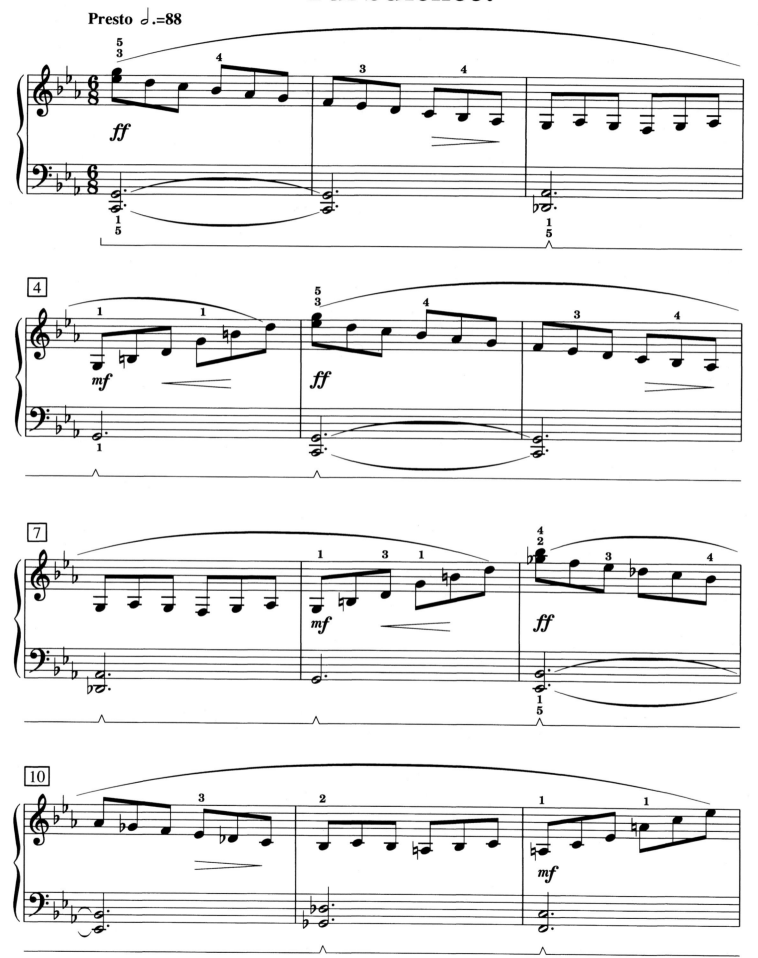

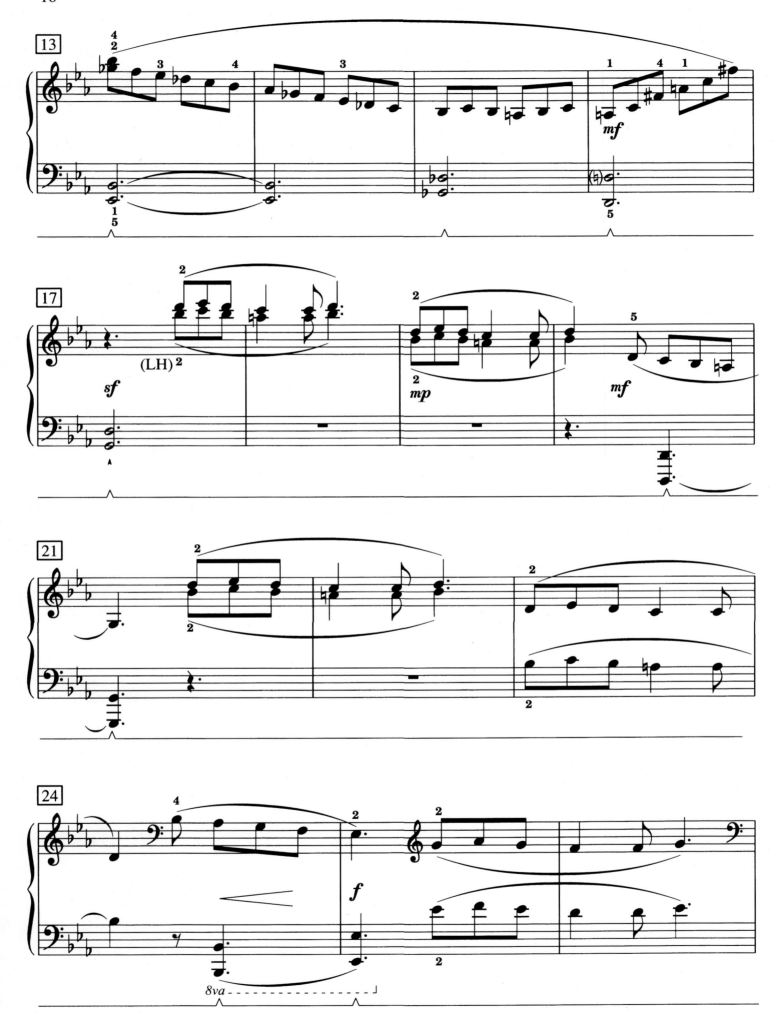

SOLITUDE

Flathead Lake, Montana

Solitude

MOUNTAIN NOCTURNE

Flathead Lake, Montana

Mountain Nocturne

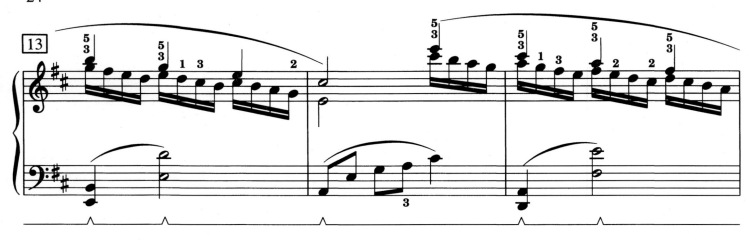

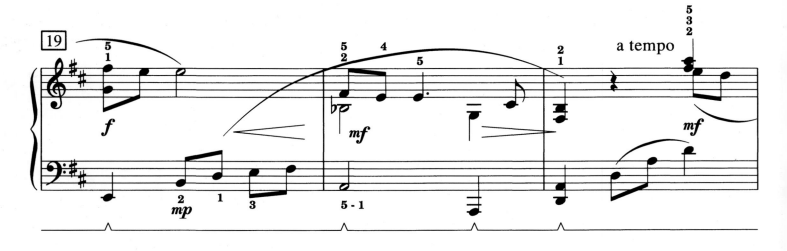

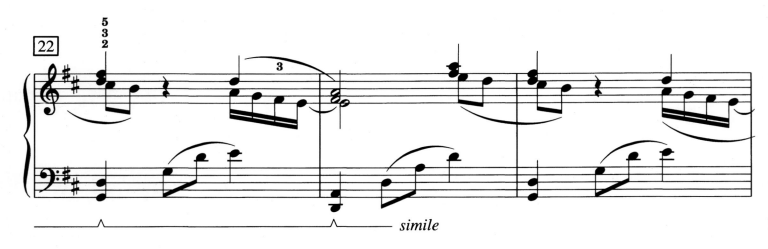

ISBN-10: 0-7390-1360-2
ISBN-13: 978-0-7390-1360-1

Alfred

alfred.com

6022 $6.95 in USA

ISBN 0-7390-1360-2